CIVIC VIRTUE
LET'S WORK TOGETHER

HOW TO TAKE INFORMED ACTION

JOSHUA TURNER

PowerKiDS press

New York

Published in 2019 by The Rosen Publishing Group, Inc.
29 East 21st Street, New York, NY 10010

First Edition

Editor: Melissa Raé Shofner
Book Design: Tanya Dellaccio

Photo Credits: Cover Drew Angerer/Getty Images; p. 4 https://en.wikipedia.org/wiki/File:Benjamin_Franklin.png; pp. 5, 22 Rawpixel.com/Shutterstock.com; p. 7 (top) Sergey Novikov/Shutterstock.com; p. 7 (bottom) PriceM/Shutterstock.com; p. 9 (Thomas Jefferson) vkilikov/Shutterstock.com; p. 9 (bottom) Monkey Business Images/Shutterstock.com; p. 11 (Edward Murrow) Hulton Archive/Getty Images; p. 11 (bottom) spatuletail/Shutterstock.com; p. 13 sitthiphong/Shutterstock.com; p. 15 SaMBa/Shutterstock.com; p. 17 (top) Mondadori Portfolio/Mondadori Portfolio Editorial/Shutterstock.com; p. 17 (Barack Obama) Steve Dykes/Getty Images News/ Getty Images; p. 19 Steve Debenport/E+/Getty Images; p. 21 (top) Chris Graythen/Getty Images News/Getty Images; p. 21 (Jimmy Carter) STR/AFP/Getty Images.

Cataloging-in-Publication Data

Names: Turner, Joshua.
Title: How to take informed action / Joshua Turner.
Description: New York : PowerKids Press, 2019. | Series: Civic virtue: let's work together | Includes index.
Identifiers: LCCN ISBN 9781508166924 (pbk.) | ISBN 9781508166900 (library bound) | ISBN 9781508166931 (6 pack)
Subjects: LCSH: Social action–Juvenile literature. | Social change–Juvenile literature. | Social service–Juvenile literature. | Research–Methodology–Juvenile literature. | Information resources–Juvenile literature.
Classification: LCC HN18.3 T87 2019 | DDC 303.4–dc2

Manufactured in the United States of America

CPSIA Compliance Information: Batch #CS18PK: For Further Information contact Rosen Publishing, New York, New York at 1-800-237-9932

CONTENTS

INFORMED ACTION

To improve life in a town, city, or country, the citizens who live there need to take action. When people take the time to learn about their communities and their fellow community members, great change is possible.

However, wanting to take action is not enough. People must also have good **information** about the world around them to take the most **effective** action possible. Being well informed is not always easy and sometimes requires a bit of work.

BENJAMIN FRANKLIN

CITIZENS NEED TO BE INFORMED AND WORK TOGETHER TO KEEP THEIR CITY IN GOOD SHAPE AND RUNNING SMOOTHLY. THE MORE YOU KNOW AND THE MORE YOU DO, THE BETTER YOUR COMMUNITY WILL BE.

CITIZENS IN ACTION

BENJAMIN FRANKLIN BELIEVED THE ONLY WAY FOR A SOCIETY TO OPERATE WELL WAS TO HAVE INFORMED CITIZENS. FRANKLIN HELPED RUN SEVERAL NEWSPAPERS DURING HIS LIFE AND MADE BEING INFORMED AN IMPORTANT PART OF LIFE IN THE YOUNG UNITED STATES.

HOW TO BE INFORMED

Being informed can take a lot of effort. It often requires reading newspapers or news sites on the Internet, talking with other informed citizens, and **developing** your own thoughts on the issues.

This all takes a lot of time. Often, people don't have enough hours in the day. Everyone has their own jobs, families, and lives to worry about. However, if you want to be the best citizen you can, taking the time to be informed is very important.

FINDING TIME TO BE INFORMED CAN BE HARD, BUT IT'S WORTH IT! LIBRARIES MAKE IT A LITTLE EASIER. THEY'RE OPEN TO THE PUBLIC AND ARE GOOD PLACES TO FIND TRUSTED INFORMATION.

NEW YORK PUBLIC LIBRARY

GOOD VS. BAD INFORMATION

Not all information is created equal. Where information comes from can be just as important as the information itself. One of the reasons you go to school is so you can get the best information possible.

Outside of school, finding good **sources** of information becomes much harder. This is especially true today. The Internet makes it quick and easy to find lots of information, but it can be hard to weed out the good from the bad.

TEACHERS DO THEIR BEST TO GIVE STUDENTS CORRECT INFORMATION ABOUT HISTORY, MATH, SCIENCE, AND MORE.

CITIZENS IN ACTION

THOMAS JEFFERSON WAS ONE OF THE FIRST PEOPLE TO PUSH FOR PUBLIC EDUCATION. HE BELIEVED EDUCATION WAS THE MOST IMPORTANT FEATURE OF A GOOD SOCIETY.

THOMAS JEFFERSON

JEFFERSON

EXAMPLES OF GOOD INFORMATION

Good information comes from many sources. Books you find in the library, **academic** journals, and newspapers such as the *New York Times* are a few of the more accepted sources of good information. People who have an area of **expertise** are also good sources of information.

Good information is about more than just the source it comes from. Good information helps you make sense of the world and can change the way you think, often in a positive way.

THE *NEW YORK TIMES* HAS JOURNALISTS, OR REPORTERS, WORKING AROUND THE WORLD, GIVING FIRSTHAND ACCOUNTS OF WORLD EVENTS. THIS KIND OF JOURNALISM IS NECESSARY TO KEEP CITIZENS INFORMED. ▶

EDWARD MURROW WAS AN AMERICAN NEWS REPORTER WHO TOOK GREAT CARE TO REPORT THE NEWS WITH TRUTH AND **INTEGRITY**. MURROW FOUGHT AGAINST THE SPREAD OF BAD INFORMATION AND WON MANY AWARDS FOR HIS JOURNALISM EXPERTISE.

EDWARD MURROW

EXAMPLES OF BAD INFORMATION

Being able to recognize bad information is an important skill, especially today. The Internet has allowed people to be more connected to the rest. However, this also means bad information is very easy to spread.

Some websites purposely share bad information, while others are not careful enough in researching what they post about. There are plenty of good sources of information on the Internet. However, incorrect or **misleading** information is often more abundant, or plentiful, and harder to **identify**.

SOCIAL MEDIA ALLOWS EVERYONE TO HAVE A VOICE ON THE INTERNET, BUT THIS CAN SOMETIMES DROWN OUT EXPERTS WHO HAVE THE BEST INFORMATION AVAILABLE.

GOOD INFORMATION LEADS TO GOOD ACTION

Being informed is just the first step when it comes to making positive changes in your community. The next step is taking action. The key to taking good action is having good information.

For example, you may want to make your classroom a better place. The best way to do this is to first become informed about your classmates and teacher. Once you have good information about what everyone in your class wants, you can work toward making change.

14

THE GOOD INFORMATION YOU RECEIVE IN SCHOOL IS KEY TO TAKING GOOD ACTION IN THE WORLD OUTSIDE YOUR CLASSROOM.

15

DIFFERENT TYPES OF ACTION

There are many kinds of action for you to take once you are informed. You could help your community by becoming an **organizer**. In this position, you'd make sure people are active in their communities on important issues.

You could also **tutor** students who need help in a subject you're good at. Helping the homeless is another way to take action in your community. If you love public service, you could even run for an elected office once you're old enough.

BARACK OBAMA LOVES PUBLIC SERVICE. HE HAS BEEN A TEACHER, COMMUNITY ORGANIZER, STATE SENATOR, SENATOR, AND EVEN PRESIDENT OF THE UNITED STATES.

CITIZENS IN ACTION

BEFORE BARACK OBAMA RAN FOR ELECTED OFFICE, HE SERVED AS A COMMUNITY ORGANIZER IN CHICAGO. THERE, HE HELPED COMMUNITY MEMBERS TAKE A STAND FOR IMPORTANT ISSUES THAT **AFFECTED** THEM.

BARACK OBAMA

CHANGE WE NEED

WWW.BARACKOBAMA.COM

CONGRATULATIONS CHICAGO'S OWN

BARACK OBAMA

PRESIDENT-ELECT OF THE UNITED STATES ★ OF AMERICA ★ -Mayor Richard M. Daley

YES WE CAN

MAKING ACTION EFFECTIVE

Once you're informed and aware of the different kinds of actions you can take, what should you choose to do? The best way to take effective action is to choose something you're interested in and love to do.

Think about the things you're interested in. There's a good chance other people in your community are interested in these things, too. Loving what you do is the key to doing it well, and this is even truer when taking action in your community.

IF YOU LOVE SPORTS, YOU CAN TAKE ACTION BY **VOLUNTEERING** TO HELP COACH YOUNGER KIDS. BY BEING INFORMED ABOUT THE SPORT AND TAKING ACTION, YOU CAN MAKE A POSITIVE DIFFERENCE IN THE LIVES OF OTHERS.

POSITIVE RESULTS

After you've taken informed action, how do you know if you've been successful? Success and positive results might not always be easy to see, but they come in many forms.

Success could be something as small as making someone smile and bettering their day. Or it could be something as large as helping to pass a new law. Success shouldn't be measured by the size of your result, but rather by the way you and those you have helped feel.

SOMETIMES INFORMED ACTION CAN LEAD TO BIG THINGS. GETTING LAWS PASSED AND SIGNED REQUIRES A LOT OF WORK AND EFFORT BUT THE RESULTS CAN BE HUGE. ▶

CITIZENS IN ACTION

AFTER SERVING AS THE 39th U.S. PRESIDENT, JIMMY CARTER HELPED GROUPS SUCH AS HABITAT FOR HUMANITY. FOR CARTER, POSITIVE RESULTS WEREN'T BASED ONLY ON THE SIZE OF HIS ACCOMPLISHMENT BUT ON THE INDIVIDUAL PEOPLE WHOSE LIVES HE COULD MAKE BETTER.

SOCIETY NEEDS YOU!

Informed action is important to make your community a better place. Whether it's the classroom you learn in or the town you live in, the well-being of your community depends on citizens taking informed action when necessary.

Always remember that action taken when it's not well informed is unlikely to be successful. Being informed and doing nothing also limits your ability to make a difference. Your community needs you, but you also need your community. When you take informed action, everyone wins.

GLOSSARY

academic: Connected with a school, especially a college or university.

affect: To change something.

develop: The act of building, changing, or creating over time.

effective: Producing a wanted result.

expertise: Special knowledge or skill.

identify: To tell what something is.

information: Knowledge or facts about something.

integrity: Honesty; the support of ideas in which you believe.

misleading: Causing someone to believe something that isn't true.

organizer: A person who helps communities focus and come together on specific issues.

source: Something that gives facts or knowledge.

tutor: A private teacher.

volunteer: To do something to help because you want to do it.

INDEX

WEBSITES

Due to the changing nature of Internet links, PowerKids Press has developed an online list of websites related to the subject of this book. This site is updated regularly. Please use this link to access the list: www.powerkidslinks.com/civicv/action

24